I0428619

JUNE 2011

# The National Institute of Justice Response to the Report of the National Research Council: *Strengthening the National Institute of Justice*

NCJ 234630

**John H. Laub, Ph.D.**
*Director, National Institute of Justice*

The National Institute of Justice is a component of the Office of Justice Programs, which also includes the Bureau of Assistance; the Bureau of Justice Statistics; the Community Capacity Development Office; the Office for Victims of Crime; the Office of Juvenile Justice and Delinquency Prevention; and the Office of Sex Offender Sentencing, Monitoring, Apprehending, Registering, and Tracking (SMART).

# Contents

Introduction ................................................... 1

My Vision for NIJ ............................................. 2

Key Accomplishments to Date ........................... 5

Recommendation #1: Ensure Independence and
Improve Governance ..................................... 6

Recommendation #2: Strengthen the Science Mission ............... 6

Recommendation #3: Bolster the Research Infrastructure ........... 11

Recommendation #4: Enhance the Scientific Integrity and
Transparency of Research Operations ........................ 12

Recommendation #5: Establish a Culture
of Self-Assessment ....................................... 14

Remaining Issues ............................................ 14

Independence ............................................. 15

Advisory Board ........................................... 15

Capacity Building ......................................... 16

Conclusion .................................................. 17

Appendix .................................................... 19

**The National Institute of Justice Response**

**to the Report of the National Research Council:**

*Strengthening the National Institute of Justice*


by John H. Laub, Ph.D.

Director, National Institute of Justice


## Introduction

The National Institute of Justice (NIJ) has welcomed the report by the National Research Council (NRC) of the National Academy of Sciences entitled, *Strengthening the National Institute of Justice*, released on July 2, 2010. The report offers a significant blueprint for NIJ to move forward as the premier federal science agency focusing on the research, development and evaluation of crime and justice topics. On July 22, 2010, I was sworn in as the Director of the National Institute of Justice. Never before in the history of the Institute has the position of Director been filled by someone with a Ph.D. in criminology and criminal justice and with extensive research experience. Some have called this a turning point for the field and it is a clear indication that science is and will be an important part of the mission of NIJ, the Office of Justice Programs (OJP) and the Department of Justice as a whole.

The NRC report offers five broad recommendations that focus on the need for independence and self-governance at NIJ, the critical elements essential for a science agency that NIJ purports to be, the need for NIJ to bolster the research infrastructure internally and externally, the need for NIJ to embrace scientific integrity and transparency in all of its activities, and the need for NIJ to embrace a culture of self-assessment (see the Appendix for the complete text of the five recommendations).

What is clear from the NRC report and is fully recognized by NIJ is the fact that the status quo is no longer acceptable. According to the NRC report, NIJ has lacked the essential tools commensurate with a science agency: a) a strong management structure, b) a scientific staff,

1

c) a budget to support both short- and long-term goals, and d) protections from political shifts. Moreover, over the last few years because of budget constraints and directives from Congress, NIJ has shifted attention and resources away from both basic and applied social science research toward capacity building and training, especially in the area of forensic sciences.

The publication of the report provides NIJ with the rare opportunity to step back and examine its core mission — where it has been, where it is now, and where it wants to be in the future. Moreover, the timing of the release could not have been better. The report gave me as a new Director the opportunity to leverage communication of my 10-point vision for NIJ with the agency's response to the NRC report. I told NIJ staff that the report imbued in me "the urgency of now," and I asked that it do the same for them. In fact, I regard many aspects of the NRC report as a blueprint for moving the agency forward in the fulfillment of many of my 10 goals.

This NIJ response to the NRC report is organized as follows: First, I present my 10-point vision for NIJ. Second, I discuss the accomplishments at NIJ over the last nine months that have strengthened the science mission. Some of these activities are in direct response to the NRC report, while others go well beyond the recommendations of the report. Third, I discuss the three issues in the NRC report that have generated the most discussion and disagreement within NIJ: what an independent science agency looks like as part of the Office of Justice Programs; the role and structure of a NIJ advisory board; and the place of capacity building for crime labs, training and technology assistance in a science agency.

**My Vision for NIJ**

As soon as I arrived at NIJ, I began articulating my vision for the Institute. In my view, this vision provides a narrative regarding what NIJ stands for and how NIJ contributes to making the world a better place. I want to give members of the NIJ community something to believe in when they come to work each day. Indeed, I want to reinforce on a daily basis the notion that NIJ provides a vital function to the field and the nation at large.

My vision includes:

1.  Respond to the National Research Council report, *Strengthening the National Institute of Justice*.
2.  Establish NIJ as the leader in scientifically based research on crime and justice.
3.  Create an organizational culture grounded in science and research.
4.  Obtain more funding for social science research and more fully integrate NIJ's physical, forensic and social science research portfolios.
5.  Develop an innovative, cutting-edge research agenda.
6.  Reach out to all stakeholders.
7.  Improve the diffusion of scientific knowledge.
8.  Ensure transparent decision-making.
9.  Improve staff morale.
10. Use everyone's talents and gifts.

Three key points deserve highlighting here. First, it is crucial that NIJ establish itself as the nation's leader in scientific research on crime and justice. For me, this means not only should our research be rigorous and scientifically sound, but it also must be of value to criminal justice practitioners — police, prosecutors, judges, correctional officials and policymakers. In my view, NIJ has a unique mission as a science agency focused on policy and practice. Given this position, NIJ faces a twofold strategic challenge — generating knowledge that is scientifically rigorous and disseminating knowledge that is useful to policymakers and practitioners.

Second, with respect to the diffusion of scientific knowledge, one of the ideas that I am emphasizing at NIJ as we move forward is "Translational Criminology." The idea of translational criminology is simple, yet powerful. If we want to prevent, reduce and manage crime, scientific discoveries must be translated into policy and practice. At the annual NIJ Conference scheduled for June 20-22, 2011, the theme is "Translational Criminology: Shaping Policy and Practice With Research." Translational criminology aims to break down barriers between basic and applied research by creating a dynamic interface between research and practice. This process is a two-way street — scientists discover new tools and ideas for use in the field and evaluate their impact. In turn, practitioners offer novel observations from the field setting that stimulate basic investigation. This is the *knowledge creation* process.

Another goal of translational criminology is to address the gaps between scientific discovery and program delivery in order to achieve effective crime policy. This is the *knowledge application* process. Translational criminology goes beyond the conventional "research to practice" idea by calling for systematic study of the process of knowledge dissemination and recognizing that successful dissemination of research findings may well require multiple strategies. Along with knowledge dissemination, we must also determine if the evidence is being implemented correctly. It is not just about finding the evidence that something works; it is figuring out *how* to implement the evidence in real-world practice settings and understanding *why* something works. Moreover, this facet of translational criminology places a priority on applicability — that is, on research with the potential for real-world implementation, something that is especially attractive in an era of limited resources.

Third, NIJ must develop an innovative, integrated, cutting-edge research agenda. By "integrated," I mean bringing together the three seemingly disparate sciences that form the foundation of NIJ — the social, forensic and physical sciences — to serve our various constituencies. I am committed to tying NIJ's programs together in a way that will give the agency's work more coherence — and ultimately improve science, policy and practice. To achieve this outcome will demand a more "visionary" understanding of the research topics that are going to be most important and useful to practitioners in the future. NIJ cannot fund research on every research question. Rather, our agenda must focus on building a cumulative knowledge base that is of the greatest value to the field. To facilitate this, NIJ needs to reinvigorate its connections with our constituency groups. One of my primary goals is to re-establish relationships with — and make NIJ's presence better known to and valued by — our key stakeholders in the research and practitioner communities, our federal partners and Congress.

**Key Accomplishments to Date**

In my second week as director, I began engaging all levels of staff in intense and frank discussions about the NRC report. I held weekly 90-minute meetings with NIJ's executive staff (the managers and supervisors of the agency) to talk about the five NRC recommendations. Parallel to this, I met every week with the nonsupervisory NIJ staff. Although I had asked each of NIJ's subunits to send a representative to these meetings, they were open to all staff, except the executive staff. I was impressed and heartened by the response. At the first meeting, for example, there were 23 people, about 40 percent of NIJ's nonexecutive staff. These parallel meetings took place over a three-month period. To have transformative change at NIJ, I believe that everyone, at all levels, must be fully engaged in the process of responding to the NRC recommendations. Both executive and nonexecutive staff prepared summaries of our discussions, which were disseminated throughout the agency. Then, I held an open meeting to discuss the two reports and to further identify points of agreement and disagreement within NIJ. It is clear to me that NIJ enthusiastically supports many of the recommendations in the NRC report. However, specific aspects of some recommendations undoubtedly warrant further discussion and these are discussed in the next section.

The larger context in which NIJ responds to this report has changed considerably since 2007 when the National Academies began its study. Beginning at his inauguration, President Barack Obama has expressed strong support for science and for the integrity and independence of federal science agencies and processes. Attorney General Eric Holder has echoed this support and has encouraged and actively supported initiatives by Assistant Attorney General Laurie Robinson to secure greater funding for NIJ and greater visibility for science in the Department of Justice. In the President's budget for 2012, this support has taken the very tangible form of a 3-percent set-aside for research and statistics — an amount that could equal NIJ's base appropriation in recent years. Moreover, within the Office of Justice Programs, Laurie Robinson has launched an agencywide evidence integration initiative to enhance our understanding about what works in reducing and preventing crime. Included in this initiative is a new Evaluation Clearinghouse/What Works Repository called the Crime Solutions Resource Center that will offer the field an online source for information about what works, what does not work and what is promising in criminal and juvenile justice programming.

In this section, I present our key accomplishments to date to strengthen the science mission at NIJ. These accomplishments are organized by the five recommendations from the NRC report.

- Recommendation #1: Ensure Independence and Improve Governance

    NIJ is already drafting proposed language for changes in statute to 1) establish clearer necessary qualifications for the NIJ Director in terms of experience with science and research, 2) modify the appointment of the NIJ Director to be a term of six years, and 3) clarify the independence of NIJ in all key aspects of its work — particularly in commissioning research and in publishing and disseminating research findings.

    As mentioned below, the peer review process at NIJ is being re-examined. NIJ has exercised its independence to implement peer review processes that reflect the best interests of science, including where appropriate exercising its independence to depart from OJP's policies on normalizing peer review scores. The importance of safeguarding the independence of NIJ on matters pertaining to peer review has been reaffirmed in a March 24, 2011, memorandum from OJP's Assistant Attorney General Laurie Robinson.

- Recommendation #2: Strengthen the Science Mission

    The NRC report argues that a successful research enterprise depends on a multiyear strategic plan that establishes research priorities and articulates a path to develop a body of cumulative research knowledge. Strategic planning should clearly describe how individual research programs are initiated, sustained, and culminated, and it must include the commitment of resources necessary to make the plan work. A research agenda signals a clear strategic plan for funding, reflects the involvement of the research field and clearly conveys agency priorities to the field.

    NIJ's strategic plan centers on translational research to transform criminal justice practice and policy. This plan has four essential components: generating knowledge, building and sustaining the research infrastructure, supporting the adoption of research evidence in practice and policy, and innovative dissemination and communication. With the goal of strengthening the science mission at NIJ, we have taken the following steps:

In February 2011, the Office of Research and Evaluation (ORE) conducted a two-day retreat to discuss strategic planning and research priorities for the office as a whole. In addition, each of the divisions within ORE — Violence and Victimization Research, Crime Control and Prevention Research and Justice Systems Research — has initiated its own strategic planning process. Each division is focusing in part on high-priority research areas within its subject areas that the agency could pursue over the next three to five years to build a cumulative base of knowledge in the field of criminology and criminal justice.

In addition, ORE convened three topical working groups of leading experts in the field to discuss existing research, emerging issues and gaps in the subject area under discussion. The first group focused on crime prevention (October 2010), the second group focused on gangs (February 2011), and the third focused on neighborhoods and crime (April 2011). Summaries of these meetings are being prepared for posting on our website.

The Office of Investigative and Forensic Sciences (OIFS) research and development (R&D) team engaged in two days of strategic planning for the R&D process and portfolio. As a result, changes were made for forensic science R&D solicitations posted for fiscal year 2011: The Basic Research solicitation was created to solicit and hopefully fund strong basic research projects that will supplement our applied research program. OIFS also added "New Investigator" qualifications in an attempt to solicit proposals from researchers in the life and physical sciences who are not currently doing research in forensic sciences. In addition, the OIFS's training solicitation was changed this year to incorporate a research component to evaluate the effectiveness of training in the forensic sciences.

The Office of Science and Technology (OST) has also taken several steps to strengthen its science mission. In particular, OST focused its efforts to realign the structure of the National Law Enforcement and Corrections Technology Center (NLECTC) System to better support NIJ's science mission and, in the process, addressed some of the concerns noted in the NRC report. The blurring of functions between the NLECTC regional centers and technology centers of excellence (COEs) was eliminated with the establishment of three regional centers in 2009 that have a research and development function. The quality of the technical and engineering support provided to NIJ's technology research efforts by the COEs was improved by a second round of COE solicitations completed in 2010. In OST, NIJ now supports four technology COEs in the areas of communications technologies, electronic crime technologies, information and sensor systems technologies, and weapons and protective systems technologies. NIJ is not completely satisfied with NLECTC System's ability to support NIJ's science mission, but progress has been made and will continue to be made.

In January 2011, the Science Advisory Board of the Office of Justice Programs held its inaugural meeting and a considerable portion of the discussion regarding my presentation to the Board focused on NIJ's research priorities and our efforts to build a cumulative base of knowledge for the field. In addition, an NIJ subcommittee of the Science Advisory Board was established. This subcommittee will provide important input and independent guidance for NIJ as it works to strengthen its science mission.

One of my goals in support of strengthening science is to create research partnerships within OJP and DOJ at large. Not only does this make sense from an intellectual standpoint, it also avoids duplication and encourages the pooling of resources and expertise. To date, several partnerships have been launched. For example, NIJ and the Bureau of Justice Statistics (BJS) have launched a joint research project, "Mining of Police Data for Statistical and Research Purposes." Also, BJS and NIJ have launched a brown bag lunch seminar series to further exchange of ideas between staff and encourage collaboration on projects of mutual interest. The Bureau of Justice Assistance (BJA) and NIJ have launched a larger and more ambitious project — a multisite demonstration field experiment of Hawaii's Opportunity Probation with Enforcement (HOPE), an innovative probation initiative designed to reduce recidivism. Along with their continuing work on research relating to offender reentry and reentry courts, BJA and NIJ are currently exploring topics of mutual interest to work on in the future. NIJ is working with the Office for Victims of Crime and the Office on Violence

Against Women on an action research project examining untested sexual assault kits. NIJ and the Access to Justice Initiative in the Department of Justice convened a workshop on a wide range of issues regarding indigent defense. And, finally, NIJ is in discussions with the Office of Sex Offender Sentencing, Monitoring, Apprehending, Registering, and Tracking about research on sex offending and with the Office of Community Oriented Policing about research on procedural justice.

Over the last several months, I have explored potential partnerships with private foundations. The partnership furthest along is with the W.T. Grant Foundation and focuses on the topic of research evidence and how it is used in the field. The idea here is consistent with the National Institute of Health's grant program, Translating Research into Practice (TRIP). However, consistent with translational criminology, I would take this a step further.

In recent months, NIJ has conducted two "listening sessions" — one with the National Governors Association (February 2011) and the second with the Justice Research and Statistics Association (March 2011). These conversations are important to NIJ because they allow us to hear directly about the areas of interest and concern to stakeholders in the field. Our plan is to continue holding listening sessions during the next year.

Over the last several months, NIJ has re-established the Institute's connection to the broader community of federal science agencies. I met with several leaders of other federal science agencies including the National Institute of Standards and Technology, the National Science Foundation, the National Institute on Drug Abuse, and the Department of Education's Institute of Science. With the Director of the Bureau of Justice Statistics, Dr. James Lynch, I met with the Social, Behavioral, and Economic Sciences subcommittee of the National Science and Technology Council Committee on Science to seek their advice on strengthening and safeguarding science at NIJ.

Since my arrival in July 2010, I have been meeting with congressional staff to discuss the science mission of NIJ and my goals and direction for the agency as we move forward. My aim is to continue fostering these relationships so that Congress has a better understanding of the value of NIJ to the field as the premier science agency working on issues concerning crime and justice.

At the core of a strong science agency is a rigorous and fair peer review process. All grants, for instance, must be awarded as the result of a fair, open, and competitive peer review process. NIJ is examining its peer review system and is currently taking the initial steps to create standing peer review panels. It is noteworthy that the use of standing panels is consistent with peer review practices at science agencies throughout the federal government. At the NIJ Conference in June, NIJ will make the formal announcement regarding its inauguration of standing peer review panels. Along with providing a stronger scientific review of grant proposals, the use of standing panels ensures improved processes and greater transparency in several ways. First, by employing larger panels of more experienced researcher reviewers, standing panels will provide better safeguards against peer reviewer bias and conflict of interest. Second, the membership of NIJ's standing review panels will be a matter of public record, as it is at the National Institutes of Health and other science agencies. This will greatly enhance transparency of NIJ's review processes. Third, standing panels (with rolling multiyear appointments of reviewers) will provide significantly greater consistency in peer review across successive solicitations and successive years.

NIJ has redoubled its efforts to develop a "culture of science" at the agency (see http://www.nij.gov/nij/about/director/welcome.htm), assuming responsibility for the prominent seminar series, "Research for the Real World" (inaugurated by OJP's Assistant Attorney General Laurie Robinson), and has brought several of the world's best researchers to NIJ to present their research work to a wide audience. (These seminars are replayed in streaming audio available on NIJ's website.) In addition, NIJ is bringing new vigor to its intramural seminar series led by NIJ staff. The new series will call on NIJ staff to make presentations on aspects of their research programs and to conduct review sessions of important published research work. Finally, NIJ's science advisor has developed a new outreach to NIJ staff to introduce them to the science mission of NIJ, including a recap of the NRC report and the way in which NIJ is responding to it.

ORE has begun the arduous task of developing standard operating procedures that will provide for consistent practices across time. These procedures will cover the gamut of ORE's work from identifying potential candidates for peer review to detailing the entire grant-making process.

NIJ has begun the challenging task of resolving the appropriate role of capacity-building programs within NIJ. Upon release of this response, NIJ will begin negotiations with OJP to transfer management of the Paul Coverdell Forensic Science Improvement Grants Program from NIJ to BJA. NIJ has begun a review of its other capacity-building activities in the areas of forensics and technology; decisions on whether these programs should continue to be managed by NIJ will be made later this year (see next section for a detailed discussion).

- Recommendation #3: Bolster the Research Infrastructure

    NIJ supports increasing resources for the purpose of further developing programs to grow the pool of researchers in all aspects related to research, development, testing and evaluation of criminal justice policies, programs and technologies. In the past, NIJ's approach to investments in the infrastructure of research (through fellowship grants, awards to young scholars, the data archive and secondary data analysis program, outreach to the research community, and other efforts) has been more substantial and better coordinated. More recently, even with limited resources, NIJ has endeavored to make significant investments in research infrastructure. It supports a widely acclaimed research and evaluation conference that brings more than 1,000 researchers and practitioners to Washington, DC, each year. Since the inception of the Graduate Research Fellowship program (which makes awards to support doctoral dissertations on criminal justice topics), NIJ has provided financial support to more than 50 criminology and criminal justice-related dissertations. In addition, NIJ's online repository of final reports and national data archive are exemplars among federal science agencies in terms of providing access to the findings and the data of government-sponsored research.

    NIJ is working to expand its Graduate Research Fellowship program to provide support across a wider range of social, physical and forensic sciences. NIJ also plans to re-establish an outreach program to graduate programs at colleges and universities, including a focus on Historically Black Colleges and Universities and other minority students.

Along the same lines, in 2010, NIJ re-established the Visiting Fellows program. (The program had been on hiatus for nearly a decade.) In addition, NIJ is considering ways to improve the current NIJ Visiting Fellows program including short-term residencies for senior criminal justice practitioners and policymakers and shared fellowships with other federal science agencies.

The NRC report recognized the scientific strength of NIJ's data archiving and secondary data analysis programs and NIJ is working to ensure the continued success of these programs. Specifically, conversations have begun with BJS regarding summer research programs and cost sharing for data archiving.

- Recommendation #4: Enhance the Scientific Integrity and Transparency of Research Operations
  As stated above, NIJ is committed to establishing and maintaining a rigorous and transparent peer review process in which applicants can have full trust and confidence. NIJ views strengthening the peer review process as the top priority in response to this recommendation, and important work has already begun regarding this matter.

With regard to NIJ reports, many problems noted in the NRC report have been addressed through a number of improvements to the National Archive of Criminal Justice Data (NACJD) and the National Criminal Justice Reference Service (NCJRS). These include an improved process for data archiving, partial withholding of grant funds to encourage submission of products, new requirements regarding submission of a data archiving strategy as part of each funding application, and improved tracking of grantee products in both NACJD and NCJRS. NIJ will continue developing and implementing other improvements such as actively identifying other grant products generated from NIJ-funded research (e.g., research articles and presentations) and improving the online experience for users of these systems. For example, the Office of Investigative and Forensic Sciences (OIFS) research and development team has implemented changes to be more transparent about the projects NIJ is funding — links to abstracts and final technical reports (completed projects) are now available at the NIJ website (http://www.nij.gov/topics/forensics/forensic-awards.htm).

Over the past few years, NIJ has taken specific steps to improve record keeping and grant management. For example, in 2010, NIJ conducted a 100-percent audit of OJP's Grant Management System (GMS) — the official grant record repository for NIJ grants. More specifically, grant files from three previous years were reviewed to ensure all required grant documentation were included in each NIJ grant file. NIJ plans to continue this review on an annual basis. In 2010, NIJ instituted monthly reconciliation meetings with OJP's Office of the Chief Financial Officer to review and align OJP's financial records and NIJ's internal files. In addition, NIJ leadership has issued supplemental guidance to NIJ staff on specific financial management and conflict of interest issues related to grants. OJP has made other improvements to GMS to provide better record-keeping processes from receipt of grant application through grant management to closeout.

NIJ will work to improve its systems for tracking projects to assess whether NIJ research programs are accomplishing their intended outcomes and to identify other needed improvements to NIJ's research programs and grant management systems. For instance, NIJ is developing a series of standard operating procedure documents for financial transactions such as interagency agreements and specific grant-processing activities (e.g., grant closeouts). The agency is conducting an inventory of all its records and is working to establish new policies on record retention. Monthly meetings with OJP's Office of Audit, Assessment, and Management are focusing on identifying and trouble-shooting specific grant actions requiring immediate resolution. NIJ continues to work with OJP to create better record keeping and greater transparency. For example, NIJ working groups are advising OJP on improvements to GMS.

In addition, one of the first decisions I made when I arrived at NIJ was to join other federal agencies in an ongoing measurement of "transparency" via Web content. NIJ will now receive a quarterly transparency rating based on Web visitors' answers to questions such as: How thoroughly does the website disclose information about what the agency is doing? How quickly is agency information made available on the site? How well can information about NIJ's actions be accessed by the public through the site? NIJ's online transparency score for the first quarter of 2011 was 82 on a 100-point scale (by comparison, the aggregate score for the 31 participating federal sites was 76.1).

Finally, we are posting periodic updates about our response to the NRC report (http://www.nij.gov/nij/about/director/strengthening-nij.htm). Along similar lines, we are considering posting progress reports or brief snapshots for a number of active grants so that our constituents can see how our research is unfolding over time rather than waiting to read the final report. These efforts encourage transparency and enhance communication with the field.

- Recommendation #5: Establish a Culture of Self-Assessment

As discussed in some detail above, in response to the NRC report, I began a series of all-staff discussions to uncover the weaknesses and shortcomings in NIJ's processes. The commitment to engage all of NIJ in developing the agency's response to the NRC report was an intentional decision that began to build a culture of self-assessment throughout the agency. NIJ continues to build on the energy that these initial planning efforts have created.

A culture of self-assessment begins with a willingness to measure the return on investment in terms of clearly established goals. New processes are being developed for regular program reviews of all NIJ's research programs. These reviews will hold NIJ accountable for establishing clear knowledge-building goals for each individual program and for making measurable progress toward achieving these goals.

I have also invited the NIJ subcommittee of the OJP Science Advisory Board to play a key role in the assessment of NIJ's work. It is my hope that the NIJ subcommittee will provide input on the research priorities of NIJ on a regular basis and will assess progress made to build cumulative knowledge in each of NIJ's areas of responsibility.

**Remaining Issues**

Specific aspects of some of the recommendations in the NRC report warrant further discussion within and outside of NIJ. There are three such issues — defining what it means for NIJ to be an "independent" science agency yet reside within the Office of Justice Programs, the role of an advisory board to NIJ and NIJ's involvement in "capacity building," which includes program activities for enhancing the efficiency and productivity of the nation's crime labs.

- Independence

Without reservation, NIJ affirms the importance of securing and sustaining the independence and authority necessary to fulfill its mission. NIJ recognizes that the principles of independence and authority are the bedrock of a science agency's programs and operations. Through statute and policy, NIJ will seek to affirm the necessary and practical independent authority in four core domains: appropriations and budget, grant-making and acquisitions, publication and dissemination and functional support operations. This will be accomplished in the next six months. We support the NRC recommendation to keep NIJ in OJP, but we will revisit this issue in two years if the necessary independence and authority needed for NIJ as a science agency is not forthcoming.

- Advisory Board

As indicated above, a new external advisory board called the Science Advisory Board has been established by the Office of the Assistant Attorney General for the Office of Justice Programs. The membership of the new OJP advisory board, which held its inaugural meeting in January 2011, was appointed by the Attorney General and includes social science researchers and criminal justice practitioners. An initial review of the composition of this group suggests that the advisory board may be inadequate to meet the diverse needs of NIJ, in large part because it lacks individuals with expertise in important research areas such as the physical sciences, technology, and forensic sciences.

This spring, a subcommittee devoted to NIJ was created including social scientists from the Science Advisory Board and three additional members were added representing the physical and forensic sciences. We are committed to working with the OJP Science Advisory Board and the NIJ subcommittee. However, we will revisit the issue of whether or not NIJ needs to have its own advisory board in two years.

- Capacity Building

The NRC report asserts that capacity-building and technical assistance programs are inconsistent with a science mission and weaken NIJ's overall commitment to science. To better strengthen its research mission, NRC recommends that NIJ cease its current work in capacity building, including the DNA and forensics capacity-building programs.[1] NIJ continues to explore specific avenues for achieving this goal, including considering whether removing capacity-building programs from its purview would, indeed, strengthen the agency's science mission. As indicated above, NIJ has initiated discussions to move the Paul Coverdell Forensic Science Improvement Grants Program to BJA. However, beyond that specific program, the link between building a stronger science mission and managing capacity-building programs is ambiguous. Certainly, NIJ can strengthen its science mission in important ways without altering its involvement in capacity-building programs; and at the same time, eliminating the responsibility for capacity-building programs would not by itself ensure stronger science at NIJ.

There may be liabilities in co-locating capacity-building or technical assistance programs within a science agency committed to advancing scientific knowledge. The integrity of the agency rests on its consistent adherence to the scientific method for prioritizing its activities, making funding decisions, and supporting "what works" (through agency publications and informing the nonscientific community, for instance). When a science agency supports capacity-building or assistance program activities that have not fully met that evidence standard nor are part of a rigorous ongoing evaluation, it may call into question the agency's commitment to scientific principles and the integrity of its scientific processes. An example of this would be encouraging forensic lab practitioners (by providing capacity-building funds) to adopt program practices or policies that have not been evaluated and are not the subject of an ongoing, rigorous research or evaluation effort.

---

[1] Although the language of the recommendation (in chapter 7) names only the DNA capacity-building program specifically, we take the thrust of the NRC report and this recommendation to include the capacity-building and technical assistance programs discussed in chapter 5, specifically the technical assistance programs that operate through the National Law Enforcement and Corrections Technology Center System.

On the other hand, NIJ's management of both research programs and capacity-building programs may provide a context for making better decisions about both research and capacity building. Having these programs co-located in a single agency may create a synergy in which each program informs the other, helping to shape better decisions about the expenditure of capacity funds, identifying the field's most pressing research needs, and developing evidence-based responses to those needs.[2]

NIJ recognizes that affirmatively deciding the best way to manage research and capacity-building programs must be a priority for the agency and the field. NIJ is committed to examining all aspects of this issue to fully resolve it and to come to an unambiguous strategy for the future. NIJ will decide this issue during the next six months.

**Conclusion**

The NRC report, *Strengthening the National Institute of Justice*, presented five important yet challenging recommendations that speak to the continued improvement and growth of the National Institute of Justice. NIJ agrees with the principles conveyed in these recommendations and has already enacted new policies and procedures that respond to the changes called for in the report. In other significant ways, NIJ has gone beyond the recommendations of the NRC report to strengthen the science mission of the agency.

It must be noted that NIJ's current funding is sufficient to fulfill only a small portion of the mission Congress has assigned to NIJ. This funding has often been used in ways that have sacrificed long-term cumulative knowledge-building in the interests of a broad "buffet" of research and other investments. The NRC report envisions a more ambitious and successful NIJ where a strategic approach builds a body of knowledge in each critical program area of the agency. Although we aspire to this model for NIJ, it is hard to see how more than a few initial steps can be taken toward

---

[2] Recent work at NIJ suggests a stronger connection between capacity building programs and evidence based research and practice than presented in the NRC Report. For example, the special report — *Making Sense of DNA Backlogs: Myths vs. Reality* — provides important empirical data to inform policy and practice. In a similar vein, NIJ staff are assessing the efficacy of collecting DNA profiles from arrestees.

this vision without a commitment of significant additional resources to support the three sciences working on research on crime and justice at NIJ. We welcome efforts from others who are concerned with achieving a more efficient and effective NIJ to help address this underlying constraint to NIJ's success as the nation's premier criminal justice research agency. By any standard, the current level of federal funding for criminal justice research fails to match the widespread and persistent challenges we face in preventing crime, managing offenders, and enhancing justice.

With a renewed sense of purpose, NIJ is ready to make great strides in providing the social, physical, and forensic science research that will be needed to make wise decisions about criminal justice policies and practices. We look forward to working with Congress, with the Administration, with the Justice Department, with our partners in the Office of Justice Programs, and with other federal, state and local partners to deliver the knowledge needed to ensure safer communities, a more effective and efficient criminal justice system, and justice for all. The intellectual challenges regarding research and practice in the areas of crime, justice and the social order are long standing and well documented. Nevertheless, these intellectual challenges offer NIJ an unprecedented scientific opportunity to advance the field.

# Appendix

**Recommendation 1: ENSURE INDEPENDENCE AND IMPROVE GOVERNANCE.** The committee recommends that Congress provide for the requisite independence and authority of the National Institute of Justice while retaining its organizational placement within the Office of Justice Programs and the Department of Justice. Among the key issues to be considered in pursuit of this goal are a statutory advisory board, a set term of office and minimum qualifications for the NIJ Director, and clear authority for NIJ to make awards and control its budget resources.

**Recommendation 2: STRENGTHEN THE SCIENCE MISSION.** To strengthen its science mission, the National Institute of Justice should direct its efforts toward building a body of cumulative knowledge that will assist the criminal justice field in its effort to prevent and control crime and improve the criminal justice system; sponsoring research that will improve and upgrade current scientific methods used to study crime; and supporting new areas that have heretofore been neglected due to NIJ's incapacity to commit resources required to support projects of long duration, great complexity, and substantial expense. To improve NIJ's ability to support research, the committee recommends that Congress remove responsibility for forensic capacity-building programs and reinstate them in other DOJ and OJP agencies, such as the Bureau of Justice Assistance and the Community Oriented Policing Services office, that have a clearly defined technical assistance mission, are closely linked to state and local criminal justice agencies, and have larger financial reserves to draw on.

**Recommendation 3: BOLSTER THE RESEARCH INFRASTRACTURE.** The National Institute of Justice should undertake efforts to nurture and grow the pool of researchers involved in criminal justice research as well as activities that support the research endeavor itself. These efforts should include increasing the resources devoted to supporting graduate education for persons pursuing a career in criminology and criminal justice studies and other disciplines engaged in research and teaching on criminal justice topics, such as the Graduate Research Fellowship Program and the W.E.B. Du Bois Program, and enhancing the Data Archive Program.

**Recommendation 4: ENHANCE THE SCIENTIFIC INTEGRITY AND TRANSPARENCY OF RESEARCH OPERATIONS.** The National Institute of Justice should revise its research operations to allow for greater transparency, consistency, timeliness, and appropriate involvement of the research and practitioner communities. In particular, NIJ should make information about its research operations and activities publicly available, easily understood, and consistent with the highest standards found in other high-quality federal research agencies.

**Recommendation 5: ESTABLISH A CULTURE OF SELF-ASSESSMENT.** NIJ should measure the influence of its programs on research and practice and assess the quality of operations and program-level technical and managerial matters.

Source: National Research Council of the National Academies. *Strengthening the National Institute of Justice*. Washington DC: National Academies Press, 2010.

## About the National Institute of Justice

The National Institute of Justice — the research, development and evaluation agency of the Department of Justice — is dedicated to improving our knowledge and understanding of crime and justice issues through science. NIJ provides objective and independent knowledge and tools to reduce crime and promote justice, particularly at the state and local levels.

NIJ's pursuit of this mission is guided by the following principles:

- Research can make a difference in individual lives, in the safety of communities and in creating a more effective and fair justice system.

- Government-funded research must adhere to processes of fair and open competition guided by rigorous peer review.

- NIJ's research agenda must respond to the real world needs of victims, communities and criminal justice professionals.

- NIJ must encourage and support innovative and rigorous research methods that can provide answers to basic research questions as well as practical, applied solutions to crime.

- Partnerships with other agencies and organizations, public and private, are essential to NIJ's success.

The National Institute of Justice is a component of the Office of Justice Programs, which also includes the Bureau of Assistance; the Bureau of Justice Statistics; the Community Capacity Development Office; the Office for Victims of Crime; the Office of Juvenile Justice and Delinquency Prevention; and the Office of Sex Offender Sentencing, Monitoring, Apprehending, Registering, and Tracking (SMART).

Our principal authorities are derived from:

- The Omnibus Crime Control and Safe Streets Act of 1968, amended (see 42 USC §§ 3721-3723)

- Title II of the Homeland Security Act of 2002

- Justice For All Act, 2004

To find out more about the National Institute of Justice, please visit:

*www.nij.gov*

or contact:

National Criminal Justice Reference Service
P.O. Box 6000
Rockville, MD 20849-6000
800-851-3420
*www.ncjrs.gov*